When the Dead Get Mail

poems by

Kasey Perkins

Finishing Line Press
Georgetown, Kentucky

When the Dead Get Mail

Copyright © 2019 by Kasey Perkins
ISBN 978-1-63534-824-8 First Edition
All rights reserved under International and Pan-American Copyright Conventions. No part of this book may be reproduced in any manner whatsoever without written permission from the publisher, except in the case of brief quotations embodied in critical articles and reviews.

ACKNOWLEDGMENTS

Several of the poems in this collection are previously published or have won prizes:

"Bloodlines," "Snowman," "The First Sign," "The Second Sign," and "The Last Sign" all appeared in *The Chariton Review* in 2014 as part of a miniature poetry portfolio.

"Bloodlines" also appeared in chapbook entitled *Those Who Breathe Once and Never Stop,* which received runner up for the Graduate Prize in Poetry at the University of Missouri St. Louis.

Finally, "Flowers from Saturn," "For a Baby Brother on his Birthday," and "Bloodlines," were recipients of the Margaret Leong Children's Poetry Prize.

This chapbook was also shortlisted for *Arcadia's* Ruby Irene Poetry Chapbook Prize contest.

Publisher: Leah Maines
Editor: Christen Kincaid
Cover Art: Kasey Perkins
Author Photo: Kasey Perkins
Cover Design: Leah Huete

Printed in the USA on acid-free paper.
Order online: www.finishinglinepress.com
also available on amazon.com

Author inquiries and mail orders:
Finishing Line Press
P. O. Box 1626
Georgetown, Kentucky 40324
U. S. A.

Table of Contents

Bloodlines 1

parens patriae 4

St. Louis: North County 6

Flowers from Saturn 9

A Game of Darts 10

The Naga Child's Transformation 11

Chicharrónes 13

Interpreting 15

When the Dead Get Mail 20

For a Baby Brother on his Birthday 21

The Tulip Period 23

In a Parallel Uterus 24

The First Sign 25

The Second Sign 26

The Last Sign 27

Fondue 28

Snowman 29

For Justin and Thalia

Bloodlines

I

We were five or six and always
ran our fingers over the bronze plaque
in your back yard, honoring the single breath
your unknown baby brother Calvin
took in this world.

Touch it,
you dared me, *it's warm.* I told you then
it was the sun.

He's an angel, you told me. Your mother
said the dead
were angels. I had never seen a real baby
or an angel, so I pictured
the only blurred image I had ever seen
of myself as a baby, nestled
in a cardboard box, asleep. My mother
said the dead
were sleeping.
My grandfather isn't an angel—
not like your brother.

This was before. This was before we knew
there was no body in the ground over which
we knelt in ritual, before we knew instead
that I was the one somewhere in a grave.

II

Ten years later you whisper to me
over a dinner of prenatal vitamins—*never,
never. I would have never
smoked meth if I had known.*

If you had known she was inside of you?

If we had known as children
that the dark red mulch around the brown
metal in the yard hid a barrenness
of ground?

Of all the grandbabies in my family
I was the only one
my grandfather ever loved.

Calvin, you tell me. Your skin is ancient,
hanging heavier than sixteen. *My mother
loved Calvin.*

But he flooded from between her legs
anyway, you say, as you chew
another pill. Your teeth are crooked.

We used to hide vitamins beneath
my old wooden dresser when
we were ten.

I run my tongue over the sharp tines of my braces.

III

Your mother begs to have her unknown
granddaughter pulled from you the way you uproot flowers.

Once, we split our thumbs
and watered the shallow furrows of flesh with
each other's blood, rubbing
red-slicked dirt
like grain seed into our bodies.

We touch. Our thumbprints slide into each other.

Is it Calvin?

That very night, I learn the photo
of the boxed baby me
was a duplicate, my underdeveloped twin
sleeping in
my grandfather's crumbling suit jacket, deep
beneath the earth.

She thinks my baby won't breathe.
She has to breathe.

I agree with your mother, but I am silent as the ground.

IV

She is an angel, you tell me. Aimya
is born, breathes once,
and doesn't stop.

We traced her name up and down
the town library—it distills
to a dozen definitions. She is a
sea of bitterness, a
wished for child. We speak nothing but
English, yet know her proximity
to the Latin *amare.*

You tell me I am her godmother.

And when she is old enough, she will look
like you. I will mistake her every day, in every face
of her grandmother's thousands of pictures.

We want to tell her everything. We want her
to feel summer inside warm bronze.

parens patriae

and then there was the commercial on the radio
that talked about lawyers for men
and it wasn't like hair

regrowth for men or like
the Commander Go Pack dietary supplements
for men

although maybe it was
it was specifically formulated for men
those in desperate need of legislative wizardry

in certain states and then
there were the children sentenced
to live with exclusively with their mother

all because she was a she and she
didn't need to fight a judge in court or
tend to a receding hairline

for that very reason, she, and the reason
we market lawyers by gender has suddenly escaped
me because there once was a girl

I went to college
with and she could piss
two hundred and fifty dollars in child

support away each month
because her mother had breasts and a mailing
address in a mom state and a propensity

for teaching her kids that a father
is nothing more than a sperm donor who ejected
his children into a cup

or her body
and that was the only responsibility he has
and that a woman doesn't need men

and then there was my father
who became broken
who made us worth forty four dollars a month

no attorneys no supplements and no
fight just one goodbye kiss
before handing us over like thirty pieces of silver.

St. Louis: North County

I

As soon as the family moved
into the broken
down Dellwood
rental,
a Blessed
Theresa of Calcutta sign
appeared in a yard
cracked,
blistered,
and dry as a communion
wafer.
Their home's lawn began
to bloom
under life
giving water
and healing hands
incased,
steady
in thrift shop garden
gloves.

II

Streets away
a Normandy man
calls 911
because he is afraid
he might
have a sexually
transmitted disease.
He is really afraid
of the St. Louis heat,
all one hundred and three

degrees, all
suffocation
and shortness of breath,
of what will happen if
he isn't admitted
to a room with air
conditioning
in time. He is afraid
that the hospital cab
won't take him
by the gas station grocery
on his way
home. He breathes
Lord, let them
take me.

III

It is two
in the afternoon:
a lone
Jennings woman sits
on her porch,
shielded in shadows cast
by neighboring
highway billboards—

a child can smile
at twenty-eight days,

the taste
of white bread
in wheat,

vote yes to the right
to work.

She is pale,
she wears khakis,
her hair
frizzes at the ends,
curls into the air
like the curls
at the end
of her cigarette—
her empty
mouth moves, twitches
around some phantom
food.

IV

Along New Florissant,
past newly
unaccredited
schools, past the beauty
shop's ninth grand
opening, past
the gas station—we
proudly accept
your EBT—every
darkened business
has the green
stamp of the
lord.

These broken
windows scream
the name of Jesus, over and
over, block after
block.

Flowers from Saturn

I paint each of you, love
Neptune's lesser known dark spot, feel
Pluto's chill in the corner of my
bedroom, near a thousand asteroid
eyes of the stuffed animals placed inside
a milky way net. The solar system
hangs from my ceiling, plastic
and precisely measured. Sirius glows
green through putty-stuck stars.

Mercury and Mars break my heart.

I search the spackled skies at night for where
my real parents might be, tucked in some
lonely part of the galaxy.

I sneak into the back yard, find Venus
with a stolen telescope, feel home just beyond
my grasp—just this flimsy atmosphere caging me
like an eyelash trapped beneath
a contact lens.

My mother is there. She has to be. She died
in some space dogfight that no one
could win, even though my father tried
to stop her.

He would bring her flowers
from Saturn. I imagine my father loving her
so much that he left me here, unable

to bear her likeness.

A Game of Darts

In their basement, he shows her how to pinch
the sharp barb of the dart in two fingers.
His hands smell
of rust and metal, the dust
that collects at the top
of the electronic dart board.

She pictures the darts as birds
whose brilliant wings soar across the room,
burying their beaks in the red,
green, and white ribbons marked with
numbers, little
cartoon creatures trapped in
the musty case.

She wears a Mickey Mouse
shirt that she will later wear to bed
while he is out forcing
a seventy-five-year-old man to his knees.

He pictures the cash in the safe, the way
the old man's face will change.

A match will be struck, its fire
bubbling and bursting
the paint from a collection of old cars
in a field nearby.

She smiles, and he
places the sharp barb in her hand.

The Naga Child's Transformation

The fever on the beach felt like the suffocating
mask of the surgeon, forcing a burst of dark
heat deep into your lungs—you slept, and I sat cross
legged beneath Florida palms. These were not
the Bodhi trees, but I wondered if you would see Manjusri
in your surgical dreams, hear him preach against
attaining enlightenment in a female body.
They were taking your breasts that day.
You signed the consent papers, fresh with your new
name, and your same softness hidden for months
under Ace bandages was to be carved away.

Thousands of years ago, when the Naga King's daughter heard
Manjusri recite the sutras, she reached her small hand
to head, removed the beautiful jewel placed between her snake-like
eyes. She gave it to Gautama, who treasured this transformation.
Your breasts went into a bucket labeled *biohazard*,
as if they were a poison growing in your chest.

I realize the *Lotus Sutra* was not written for us. The rabbi
at our wedding cannot know. He cannot know that beneath
the chuppah, beneath your tallit, your body has been
molded from old clay, the dark place between your legs sealed
up like a cave. I thank God for the heart
attack that took my father before I knew you.

The sutras do not tell us if the Naga King was proud of his
daughter-turned-son, of her yearning to treat her body like a wisp
of smoke, a handful of mud to mold. Your father
had always wanted a son, but not like this. *Never like this*,
he said, though he clenched your mother's hands tightly
in his, took the steps into the hospital.

When your wounds heal, we will take another step. We will travel from hospital to hospital like those monks in saffron robes, seeking your enlightenment, a promised land, a negation of self for your body. But for now I trace the thick, pink ropes of tissue beneath your nipples, the scars like snakes—twisted and alive. My ear rests against your hardened chest.

Chicharrónes

It didn't occur to me until later,
peeling back the fatty skin
of a roast chicken on chicken
verde night, that "pork
rinds" is such a strange term.

I saw these made from scratch
on the television earlier, where most
such cooking gets done. I saw
Aarón Sánchez salivate
over chicharrónes, saw Guy Fieri gasp
at pork parts plunged
into a deep fryer,
bursting into being like a
bacon star going nova, swept
with a comet-like dusting
of salt and bits of lime.

I pull the skin from flesh with
a chef's knife, imagining
the rind of a lemon, lime. Pork
rinds? As if the gentle pig
were a mango with legs, an orange
rooting for mushrooms in
my backyard. Do I zest Wilbur?
Do I shred his citrus pith with
the microplane I got for
Christmas? Pork rinds—

as if my own flesh would peel
back to reveal luscious grapefruit
quarters. And PETA—I wonder now how

they have not made this poster
as I take a peppered, dripping swath
of chicken rind from pot and place
it on my human tongue, feel
grease on my sentient skin sheets—

I picture the picket sign: labeled
pork rinds, it features the
dimpled flesh of a human: its zest,
perfectly prepped.

Interpreting

I

He clung to her legs,
arms wrapped tightly as roots
choking the ground, and begged
for hicken,

*can we have it, please,
please,*

boy drug across the tile
floor of the kitchen, while she stared
into a refrigerator

coated with smears of ketchup
and a long, thin Coca Cola
stain that branched out
into the little fridge ridges like
his small, grasping fingers.

I'm parvin'.

II

He don't know nothin' 'bout talkin'.

My mother would tell the
raccoon-eyed woman
every night,
the one with the glamour shot hair
who lived behind the bar.

My younger brother and I
let our feet dangle
against the rail
that kept the stools from bashing
the clean
polished wood front.

He talk real dutchie.

We kicked each other beneath the
whiskey-holding overhang,
kicked 'til our shins bruised.

III

It took me until I was ten to realize
the Dutch were surely all drug addicts—
the song in the car
sang to us, saying

pass the dutchie 'pon the left-hand side—

but still I wondered
how you could hold my brother's
broken speech
in your hands and pass
it along, like gossip, or something
you could tinker with.

Our older brother was the one
who finally sat us down
for the talk.

You dump the tobacco first

and then add everything else,
Ryon said,
rolling it around, tongue lolling
against paper
like our St. Bernard did in the back yard
with the garbage.

You gotta get it wet
with spit
so it sticks.

You're good at this.

IV

Back then,
I wanted to help,

so I looked at my mother—
square in the eyes—
my feet rooted to the tile floor,
fingers braided
with my brother's.

He wants chicken. He is hungry.

It became a talent.

I'm good at this.

V

Well howdy, Parvin'
I'm your dad,
our father would say, and
and laugh
and shake
my brother's hands as tears rolled
down his small face.

He is hungry.

We fought with swords in the
cramped bedrooms—sticks sharpened
to points, old two
by fours from the dump wrapped
and attached
with vines for hilts.

His face glowed with excitement
as he screamed *hoard fight!*
and came at me,

birch tip
aimed to eye,
hands rubbed raw from
poison ivy vines.

VI

We went to *fucky hicken*
one night
to have some of the Colonel's finest.

I played in my mashed potatoes,
told our parents that
chocolate squirrels
were ice cream and that
I was parving too.

When the Dead Get Mail

When the dead got mail, my father used to take the envelopes between his teeth and tear them apart. The paper spilled across the kitchen tile like little snowflakes. When the dead got mail, he talked to us, about the man whose first, middle, and last were torn to pieces on the floor—you have your grandfather's name, he told us. He used to make us mayonnaise and baked bean sandwiches as kids. When my grandfather received *Playboys* from beyond the grave, we always kept them.

He once got so drunk at your uncle's high school graduation that he passed out in the bleachers.

I am passed out on the couch when the dead get mail for the first time at my house. You've been gone for two years—my grandfather, decades. But I can think only of your skin, wasted and yellow, when I hold this smooth mailer in my hands. One piece, unmarred, from Dell, will sit for weeks in the metal box by my front door. It begs you in large letters to come back soon.

For a Baby Brother on his Birthday

We told you that people who were born
on Tax Day were cursed—those first
nursed on the day Lincoln pulled a bullet
into his brain, those
brought into the world with the
unsinkable Titanic flickering
on their silver screen faces—
you, once beaten into submission
for spilling Cheetos across our bathroom
floor, pasty orange curls cascading
on tile like the mullet of blond ringlets
spilling over your dirty neck.

What you don't know:
I once created a program to read
your emails when you were fourteen.

You slept on a park bench that December,
you stole and sold our mother's stolen
prescription pills,
you once tied a broken condom
in a knot and put it back on—

here I was, thinking I would simply check to see
if you were doing your homework.

April the fifteenth comes,
cruelly, and I see the shadow
of that raised hand cast across
a cheese dusted floor; I see the shadow
of pinstripes on your face,
like a nice suit for court. I see the shadow
of your own hand
scrawled across the yellow
legal pad paper.

Your words are misspelled. Your letter 'p' still
looks the way I taught you to write it,
one loop and a little tail, at the kitchen table
playing school together.

Little brother—once, when you were six
you watched Leonardo DiCaprio
sink into the Atlantic and you asked me
if it was your fault.

The Tulip Period

The Ottoman Empire once enjoyed a peace
named for their tulips—for armfuls of years and
leisure in riotous color.

Our dog Isabeau celebrates

this season—she springs through the April light,
burrows through to follicles of dirt, returning
to our side with a bulb clenched in canines—

and you shudder.

I know this tulip—I know
it is for your first, I know she is purple
and orange, stamens that still

blink in our backyard, and I shudder.

I am green. I pull you to me and think of Istanbul—
when everyone came home
to notebooks, lovers, flowers

by the thousands, candlelit—

I feel it even now, in Missouri,
where last week's springtime snow
choked the buds that float

in the white sea of our yard.

In a Parallel Uterus

Dreams of our future baby still drift through
me as I walk the steps to the
Florissant courthouse—she had been
born with a head of dark, sweet
tufts, your lush lips with a touch
of my heart shaped peaks.

I wait in line while the woman far ahead
of me stands, a car seat
at her feet, paying over seven hundred
dollars in various violations—
a bill for each week
of her son's life.

"Momma ain't goin' jail
no more," she assures him sweetly, and
when she drops a final fiver
on the countertop, the boy in the basket
begins to choke, all glazed
eyes and warm milk bubbles that burble over
his smooth, fat chin.

"Stop it, you," the woman says, as she shakes
her son's tiny universe by its handle,
hard, his small arms wind milling,
almost overturning
his round body onto tile which, now that I look
at it, is the same shade of grey as
the eyes of last night's

somnambulant child, the weight of our
imagined daughter's
soft form lifting from feet—from
the last of my sleep,
replaced only with the parking ticket
clutched tightly in my hand.

The First Sign

He wakes in a cold dark,
underscored with a line of cooling urine
that seeps into his *Toy Story* bed sheets.

He cries for his mama.

You're too old for this.

Light splits the room, and her frame
warms the same swath of wet
shame.

You'll never be a big boy. Ever.

She pushes his small body into the ocean
of the mattress, his breath catching
like a diver just breaking the water barrier,
its surface tension a slap.

He soaks it all in—the pressure
of her hands. The digging acrylic nails.

The scent of piss.

The Second Sign

He learns how to make fire
from his first and only
day as a Cub
Scout. Toilet paper doesn't hold
together
the way sticks do, doesn't create
a perfect
teepee to shelter
his blaze
from the ceiling fan above.

He shelters his spark with his body,

strikes match after match, the flames
like bursts of birds diving
into a field—
flames straight
into the grain-like hills of beige
carpeting
and quilted white ribbons.

And oh, how the ribbons wither
joyously
to nothing,

and oh, how his face withers,
caught, when she walks
into the living
room.

The Last Sign

he rips the bulb
broken
from its watery world
algae slick
like his blood
on the glass and grit
he grabs
its tiny scaled body
fins flap in hands
he feels
its cold fluid
filled lungs expand
in panic
collapse in resign
expand again
he feels
the scales sink
into his hands' creases
he squeezes
and its eyes
bulge golden
mouth golden
gasping
fish breath
and his
breath
and for
one second no one
is there
just one boy
and one fish
birthed into air.

Fondue

Put the cheddar in first. Everyone has cheddar—it will be the bag at the back, half unzipped, like a secret impulse. The tops of its shreds will feel like age hardened fingernails against your skin, against your soft and better instincts. Use only chorizo. American anything will simply never cut it. The cloves in the chorizo will supplement the processed cheese product like a smooth shot of Crown Royal sweetens a cheap cigarette. Use chives. Use them the way you use cocaine—sparingly, perhaps. Pour everything you have into the pot. Everything to taste.

Snowman

You have to pack the center,

I tell you,

as your palm opens for me
like the icy cherry
blossoms falling from
the sky, and I
place a frozen diamond
in your glove.

*He has to have a strong
core before you
can wrap him in snow skin—*

just then, our elderly neighbor
across the street peeks
her face from her screen
door, delighted
to see children playing
in the midnight snow.

Start here.

Last night we talked in
the truck under trees
with leaves of
pearly cold, and you told me
you couldn't wait
to get married.

I need you,

as I laugh at a snowball
too large to push up
the front yard,
laugh at the neighbor
chuckling her way back
inside—

we children, married
twice
to different people,
different lives, and I

am dying to do it again.

But you had never made
a snowman,
so in this new land
of firsts we stack white
boulders in the night,

and as we lean to kiss
each snowy cheek
of our newly frosted friend,
I feel you
through two feet
of compacted flakes,

one o'clock in the morning
pressing upon us like lips.

Kasey Grady, who publishes under Kasey Perkins, is a teacher, freelance editor, and writer who completed her MFA in poetry from the University of Missouri - St. Louis in 2014. She also holds a MA in English with a focus on writing pedagogy and a BA in English with a focus on composition, both from Truman State University. During her time in Kirksville, MO, she was both a frequent performer and organizer in the poetry slam community. Overall, her poetry and poetry book reviews have appeared in the *Chattahoochee Review, Chariton Review, Digital Americana, the Wisconsin Review, the Oracle, Lumina*, and many more. Her poetry has won some prizes, such as the 2014 Margaret Leong Children's Poetry Prize, and has been shortlisted for others, such as the Arcadia Ruby Irene Poetry prize.

In addition to teaching first year writing and foodways courses at Washington University in St. Louis, she serves as the faculty advisor for WuSLam, the university poetry slam team. Her scholarly interests include memoirs, food writing, writing pedagogy, and pop culture adaptations of literature. When not engrossed in the world of reading and writing, she loves to cook, entertain, watch bad television, and spend time with her husband Justin, daughter Thalia, and two rescue dogs.

www.ingramcontent.com/pod-product-compliance
Lightning Source LLC
LaVergne TN
LVHW041510070426
835507LV00012B/1459